How To Conduct
Performance
Appraisals

by Bob Klein

Dedication

I would like to thank my wife, Lynn, for her patience, encouragement and support while I was writing this book.

I would also like to thank the Publications Committee and the Board of Directors of the Professional Society for Sales and Marketing Training".

Having attended (SMT) functions for the last ten years and being an active member for the last eight years, I have found it to be a very beneficial and valuable organization. In fact. I feel (SMT) is essential to anyone involved in Sales and Marketing Training.

Bob Klein (All rights reserved)
E-mail: robtklein@aol.com

CONTENTS

PREFACE

This book is targeted for Sales Managers, District Managers, Regional Managers, Divisional Sales Managers and/or Vice Presidents of Sales. It will benefit all those who are interested in, or responsible for, the management and supervision of Sales People.

To survive and prosper in today's competitive business environment, a company must possess a highly productive work force producing and selling high-quality products and services. Performance Appraisals can help achieve these goals by promoting understanding between Sales Managers and Sales Reps, regarding job expectations and by providing guidelines for improving performance through feedback and establishing specific Developmental Action Plans.

The objectives of this book are as follows:

After reviewing and studying this booklet, readers will be able to:

1. Describe the three parts of the Performance Appraisal Cycle.

2. Write clearly defined and measurable performance expectations.

3. Explain Performance Ratings.

4. Conduct effective Performance Planning, Feedback, and Appraisal sessions and design specific Developmental Action Plans

5. Explain the Sales Reps Role in the Performance Appraisal Cycle.

BOB KLEIN

FORWARD

Of all the training programs I've designed and delivered over the years, none of them stir the emotions of both participants and trainers as much as the subject of Performance Appraisals.

Sitting in judgment and evaluating the performance of others is not a skill or talent with which people are born. It has to be learned.

And the only way to learn it Is to practice, practice, practice.
This booklet contains information from numerous books and
articles of "experts" in the subject of Performance Appraisals along
with my practical experience as follows:

1.   Eight years as a Sales Rep "carrying the bag."
2.   Twelve years experience in line sales management.
3.   Thirty years in corporate training and development.
4.   Thirty years as a university professor teaching courses   like: Salesmanship, Sales Management, Marketing and Human Relations in Management.
5.   I have also developed company-wide performance management systems.

Writing this book on Performance Appraisals has been a labor of love for me. I happen to believe that the only way for organizations to effectively ac-complish their objectives is for Sales Managers and Sales Reps to work very closely together to:

1.   Establish clearly defined, measurable performance expectations.
2.   Communicate frequently, and on a continuous and on-going basis, about the status of these expectations and agree on the means for achieving and exceeding them.

3.   Meet face-to-face at least once a year to formally appraise performance and design Sales Rep development activities to enhance future performance.

I hold a strong belief that the organization's goals and objectives are not mutually exclusive from the individual's goals and objectives. The "Organization" is a "Vehicle" that Sales Reps can ride. They can accomplish their personal goals and objectives by helping the company accomplish its goals and objectives.

Moreover, I believe the "Partnership" between Sales Manager and Sales Person should be very strong. To me, it's analogous to a person trying to keep their balance while walking down a Single railroad rail. They're a little unsteady and off balance. But if their manager is walking down the parallel rail, and the two of them clasp hands in the middle, they can proceed down the track with much more stability on the way towards achieving their destination. Sure, they'll have to be making minor course corrections, and this will require constant communications. But the likelihood of them reaching their goals will be much increased. The resulting teamwork endeavors and open communications will also provide a much more satisfying work environment that will enhance the quality of work life for all concerned.

I think the two most powerful motivators of human behavior are, in this order:

"Achievement and Recognition."

The systems and procedures recommended in this booklet regarding Performance Appraisals should help Sales People and Sales Managers attain both.

Good Luck and Good Selling.

SECTION 1: A POWERFUL MANAGEMENT TOOL

One of the most hated jobs of any Sales Manager is that of conducting Performance Appraisals. They complain that this responsibility forces them into the roles of "Judges" and "Police Officers." In reality, if done correctly, Performance Appraisals can become a Sales Manager's most powerful management tool. All that is required is for Sales Managers to shift their thinking from being "Judges" and "Police Officers" to becoming "Enhancers" and "Coaches." If Sales Managers can incorporate into their thinking the notion that they should serve primarily as "Resources" for their Sales People who want to improve their performance, they will be able to reap immediate benefits. And if they can serve more as "Coaches" instead of trying to enforce the law, they can create more of a "We" feeling instead of "You vs. Me."

Another important shift in thinking that would help Sales Managers would be if they started asking their Sales People to serve in a "Partnership" relationship with them. Managers should make Sales People "Partners" in establishing objectives and managing their own performance to achieve those objectives.

The Performance Appraisal Program should be a joint process in which the Sales Manager and Sales Person seek to communicate clearly about the job, the employee's performance and develop action plans for enhancing future performance. It should be a mutually beneficial experience designed to improve the quality of work life and make your organization a more satisfying place to work.

While performance management can be a valuable tool in helping organizations accomplish their objectives, the vast majority of companies feel their performance appraisal systems are ineffective. Reporting in a recent issue of *Journal of Compensation and Benefits.*, Elaine Evans said:

"Only 14 percent of 3,000 companies recently surveyed feel that their current performance management systems are effective. "

If that's the case, why do so many performance appraisal systems fail? In responding to this question, Bob Losyk reported in the:

Credit Union Executive:

"Performance appraisals often fail because supervisors don't understand what constitutes good performance. Nor do they know how to discuss performance with employees face-to-face. No interview can produce positive results without adequate preparation and a commitment to back up words with specific actions."

In the same article, Mr Losyk presented the following list of why performance appraisals fail:

WHY PERFORMANCE APPRAISALS FAIL

- No face-to-face discussion.
- No preparation by either party.
- No follow-up.
- No knowledge of performance or how to appraise it.
- Insufficient identification of performance problems.
- Inadequate communication about performance during the period being appraised.
- Biased ratings.
- No connection between ratings and actual performance.
- No relationship between performance objectives and the appraisal form.
- Concern only with poor performance.
- Annual, rather than continuous appraisal.
- Excessively complicated appraisal forms.

BENEFITS:

The benefits of implementing and utilizing an effective Performance Management Program are numerous. To begin with, an integrated Performance Planning, Appraisal and Development system can be created to:

- Promote understanding between Sales Managers and Sales People about the organization's performance expectations and the means for achieving them.
- Motivate Sales People to achieve higher levels of performance.
- Link financial rewards to the achievement of current performance expectations.
- Enhance Sales Rep's morale by giving timely feedback and assistance in improving performance.
- Support Sales Rep's development with specific Developmental Action Plans and Progress Review Dates.

So, if done properly, Performance Appraisals could provide:

BENEFITS OF A GOOD PERFORMANCE APPRAISAL SYSTEM

1. Improved sales performance

2. More bottom line profits

3. Better customer relations

4. Larger market shares

5. Reduced turnover

6. Improved morale

7. Better communications between Manager and Sales Rep

8. Higher caliber Sales People

Many new Sales Managers think that the only Real performance measure that is important for Sales People is "Hitting their sales numbers."

This is a popular misconception. Sales People need to be measured and rewarded/acknowledged for more than just the "sales numbers." Other important job responsibilities and outcomes should also be stressed. This includes things such as the following:

RESPONSIBILITIES OTHER THAN SALES

THAT SHOULD BE MEASURED AND RATED

1. Customer relations
2. Market shares
3. Promotional activities
4. Cooperation with team members
5. Training new Sales Reps
6. Selling the entire product line
7. Inventory control
8. Posting sales records
9. Collections
10. Following up on paperwork, reports, etc.

BOB KLEIN

SECTION 2: HISTORICAL PERSPECTIVE

Appraising and managing performance is not new. In a recent issue of *Records Management Quarterly*, Henry Pratt said references to performance management were found in the Wei Dynasty in China dating back to the third century A.D. While performance management theory and practice in the U.S. started with the Industrial Revolution in the late 18th century, the widespread use of performance appraisal techniques with blue collar employees didn't appear until after W.W. I. Appraisal systems for measuring managerial, professional and sales employees weren't used extensively until the latter part of last century.

The earliest appraisal programs during the Industrial Revolution were rather crude and simple. Workers were evaluated and paid primarily on the basis of quantity output - the number of "pieces" they satisfactorily turned out.

It was not until later that management recognized that in many jobs, the quality of work produced also affected an individual worker's impact on the organization. At that time, evaluation procedures and compensation plans were enlarged to incorporate work quality, in addition to quantity.

Workers' output gradually shifted from directly-measurable physical activity to more complex tasks requiring the application of greater Skills, Knowledge, Aptitudes and Personal Characteristics (SKAP's). That's when more measurable performance standards/expectations or yardsticks became necessary. At first, these yardsticks were quite subjective in nature, and were typically based on the manager's assessment of the attitudes and personality traits seen in workers.

The attitude and personal1ty assessment was then combined with the manager's overall evaluation of qual1ty and quantity of work produced.

Among the attitude and personality traits assessed were such ambiguous elements as loyalty, honesty. Initiative, cooperation, resourcefulness, teamwork, ambition, etc. Many of the early appraisal programs also covered elements like attendance, punctuality, following instructions, accepting responsibility, adherence to rules and regulations. etc.

So early performance measures were often highly subjective and allowed raters too much personal latitude. Management needed a more effective way of appraising employee performance that would emphasize more job relatedness and easier measured elements that addressed the quality and quantity of work.

MANAGEMENT BY OBJECTIVES (MBO)

When the idea of Management by Objectives (MBO) became **widely used in the latter part of the 1900's,** management looked to MBO to provide a more meaningful way to appraise employee performance. The idea was based on goals. where employees would accept and commit themselves to achieve certain predetermined goals in line with those of the organization.

Were these types of goal-striving programs effective? It was obvious that these programs had certain strengths. But they also had their limitations.

Since goals and objectives are primarily forecasts of what could be achieved, employees soon recognized that a variety of external influences might affect actual job achievement. Sometimes the boss made allowances for these external events, such as budget cutbacks, abrupt job priority changes, highly unusual competitive activities, or adverse economic conditions. At other times, employees were unfairly held responsible for conditions that were beyond their control. Obviously, this would not be an acceptable situation.

EMPLOYEE INVOLVEMENT

It soon became apparent that it's critical to the success of a Performance Appraisal Program to involve employees in the establishment and later revisions (if necessary") of performance objectives and/or expectations. By giving employees the opportunity to playa meaningful role in establishing and/or revising goals, management can obtain a greater understanding, commitment and support for the objectives to be achieved. Employees will have a greater sense of "ownership" of the goals because they will have been involved in establishing them. It's not something that has been imposed upon them from "above."

SELF ANALYSIS QUIZ

The Self Analysis quiz that follows is designed to show you how well you are using goals in your organization. It was presented in an article in the Morristown, N.J. *Daily Record* Newspaper. The article was written by Professor Gerald Graham of Wichita State University. Please answer each question being as truthful as possible. Without lengthy deliberation. just mark the answer that is most appropriate: either "Very Confident," "Somewhat Confident," "Somewhat Uncertain," or "Very Uncertain."

SELF ANALYSIS
HOW WELL DO YOU USE GOALS?

Put a check (✓) in the appropriate square.

	VERY CONFIDENT	SOMEWHAT CONFIDENT	SOMEWHAT UNCERTAIN	VERY UNCERTAIN
1. All of my departmental goals are specific and tangible.				
2. I have no trouble identifying my top three departmental goals.				
3. My Sales People can tell me precisely how well we are accomplishing each of our three top goals.				
4. If asked to rank our goals, my Sales People would rank our top three goals in the exact same order as I do.				
5. My manager would agree completely with my top three goals.				
6. I have regular meetings with my Sales People to talk about goals.				
7. All of my Sales People have a written copy of our top three goals.				
8. In all decisions, my first thought is how this will serve our goals.				

SCORING: Now rate yourself on how well your organization uses goals to accomplish its objectives. For every "Very Confident," give yourself 4 points; for every "Somewhat Confident," 3 points; for every "Somewhat Uncertain," 2 points; and 1 point for each "Very Uncertain."

26+:	You have very effective use of goals;
20-25:	Good, but could improve
19 or Less:	Could use goals much more effectively

SECTION 3: LEGAL ASPECTS

In a recent issue of Personnel Management:

Professor Barbara Townley of the University of Alberta discussed the legal aspects of managing employee performance in her article. "A Discriminating Approach To Appraisal."

She offers some guidelines for avoiding litigation and making a company's position more defensible if ever an employee dispute is tested by the courts.

Given the subjective judgments of many Performance Appraisal Programs. discrimination is bound to creep in. Human Resource professionals have been forced to deal with this fact as a result of decisions by the courts.

U.S. Government-issued uniform guidelines set standards for hiring procedures and employment testing. (e.g .. E.E.O. guidelines and Affirmative Action Policies.) Where selection procedures have an "adverse impact" on minority groups. the employer must provide evidence that these procedures are job related. Performance Appraisals are now defined as being generic employment tests and are therefore subject to the same scrutiny.

An adverse impact would be established if there was a statistically significant difference between the average appraisal scores of minority and nonminority groups.

Court decisions have addressed the important issues of the "Who", "What", and "How" of appraisals as follows:

WHO SHOULD RATE PERFORMANCE?

The courts have agreed that appraisers need to be familiar with the work involved and have therefore generally favored first-line managers as appraisers.

WHAT SHOULD BE APPRAISED?

Courts have decided that ratings must be "Rational" and well-considered, usually based on pre-established and well communicated standards. The emphasis is therefore on systematic evaluation based on predetermined criteria and openness, in the sense that criteria used in assessment are well-defined and known by both managers and their employees.

Courts have generally found against those systems using "Subjective" criteria based on characteristics such as:

"Adaptability, bearing, Demeanor, manner, maturity, drive, leadership ability, intelligence, appearance, cooperation, dependability, stability, etc."

In cases involving pay increases, promotions. etc., criteria are to be related as closely as possible to job outcomes. The more objective these outcomes are, the more defensible the procedure is. The tendency seems to be towards close attention to job content in establishing performance objectives as well as an emphasis on concrete observable performance.

HOW SHOULD APPRAISALS BE HANDLED?

The courts have stressed the need to train appraisers. Particularly the way managers handle protests. Opportunities to discuss assessments with the appraiser and for the latter to be able to appeal have been supported and decisions reversed where these conditions have not been met. Where provisions for dissent or appeal are available but have not been taken up by the appraiser, the courts have tended not to find in favor of a plaintiff.

Some of these decisions have dramatic implications. As D.C. Martin observed in the Employee Relations Law Journal, vol. 12, no. 2, 1986, "Given the importance of performance appraisals, it is surprising that the performance appraisal methods and systems within which they are embedded are not attacked more often."

Organizations would be wise to adopt the following recommendations to avoid potentially discriminatory appraisal procedures:

1. Criteria should be job-related, preferably developed from job analyses, identifying behaviors rather than personal traits, and have precise rather than vague standards.
2. There should be a check on appraisers through a review by the next level of management.
3. There should be evidence of the system being valid and reliable.
4. There should be provisions for open discussions on the evaluation with the employee, with the latter having the opportunity to question or challenge any written comments.
5. There ought to be an opportunity for appeal.
6. Employees should have written guidelines on how to complete appraisals, including Equal Employment Opportunities awareness.

7. There should be adequate provisions for follow-up opportunities, access to training courses, developmental assignments, etc.

In summary, Performance Appraisals, when conducted in the legal context described here, can influence important organizational outcomes such as performance and satisfaction. It's important that Performance Appraisals and Reviews do not take place in a vacuum, but occur within the context of the interpersonal relationships between Sales Managers and their Sales People. The content of an appraisal (the Sales Person's opportunity to participate in the discussion, the criteria on which the performance evaluation was based, and the discussion issues important to the Sales Person's development) is, in part, a function of the Sales Person's and the Sales Manager's ongoing interpersonal relationship.

Done right, a performance evaluation can be just as valuable as a day of training or a semester of continuing education. Too often, Sales Managers lose sight of the process's fundamental purpose in the storm of paperwork and compensation concerns. The ideal of the Performance Appraisal is to improve on-the-job performance. It is the most effective tool available for altering a Sales Person's behavior.

SECTION 4: THREE PARTS OF THE PERFORMANCE APPRAISAL CYCLE

The steps involved in appraising a Sales Rep's performance should consist of a simple process designed to enhance Sales Manager and Sales Rep communications about performance and development. It should emphasize the <u>COMMUNICATION</u>, not the structure or the paperwork.

The process is one of continuous communication, but it can be thought of as three sequential steps as illustrated below:

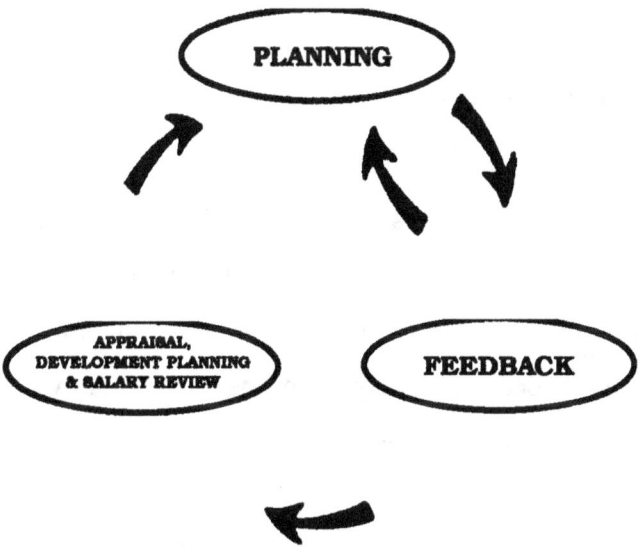

The Three Steps are as follows:

• **PERFORMANCE PLANNING:** This is where the Sales Manager and the Sales Rep meet to discuss and agree upon the specific criteria under which performance will be evaluated during the year. It should be conducted once a year, usually at the beginning of the Performance Appraisal year. There should be a shared understanding of exactly WHAT is to be accomplished, WHEN it should be accomplished and

HOW WELL it should be accomplished in as specific and measurable terms as possible.

NOTE: It's very important that the Sales Manager's manager be brought into the loop as early as possible. This is to ensure that what the Sales Manager and Sales Person agree on has already been "Blessed" from above. This should prevent disagreements when the year-end review is conducted. During the yearly Performance Planning Meeting, the Position Description should be reviewed, and revised, if necessary.

• **FEEDBACK SESSIONS:** This is where the Sales Manager and the Sales Rep get together periodically to discuss how performance is tracking against the agreed upon expectations established in the Performance Planning meeting. The arrow pointing back towards Planning indicates that agreed-upon performance expectations could be, and should be, revised as changing situations dictate. These feedback sessions should occur quarterly, monthly, weekly, or even daily, to ensure continuous, on-going communications.

• **APPRAISAL, DEVELOPMENTAL PLANNING & SALARY REVIEW SESSION:**

This is where the Sales Manager rates the past year's performance against expectations, determines the merit salary increase and gets agreement from the Sales Rep on Development plans and progress review dates. (Some companies prefer to hold the salary discussion for another meeting to separate discussions about performance from discussions about money.) The process begins again with performance planning for the coming year.

SECTION 5: ESTABLISHING MEASURABLE OBJECTIVES

Sales Rep and Sales Manager should come to a shared understanding of the important parts of the job and the specific ways in which satisfactory performance of each job responsibility will be measured. Once that's been accomplished, they need to make sure no job changes have been overlooked. It's a good idea to review definitions and expectations at the time of each performance feedback discussion.

This is the heart of a Performance Appraisal Program. If planning is done right, it will make all the other steps easy.

Establishing performance objectives is similar to establishing sales call objectives. Most Sales Managers already know how to set good sales call objectives, because they had to master this skill to be successful when selling. It should be a relatively easy task to transfer this skill to the managing of their sales team.

There's a straightforward way to arrive at workable expectations - through the use of these simple procedures:

    A. State results in specific time frames.

    B. Make sure results are measurable and attainable.

    C. Get commitment.

First, using specific time frames: In setting an expectation, it's important that time, be considered. Planning or success means making commitments to achieving results by a certain date. Often expectations are thought of as being set for one year. But it's just as feasible to set them in other time frames such as a quarter, six months, etc. Whatever the appropriate time-frame, it should be stated as a part of the expectation.

Second, measurable and attainable: Wherever possible, expectations should be measurable. Here again, numerous measures may be feasible as long as Sales Manager and Sales Rep have a shared understanding about them. Time, quantity, quality, accuracy, dollars, economically, consistency, behaviors, safety, etc., should be used so expected results are as specific as possible.

GUIDELINES FOR WRITING EXPECTATIONS

Expectations are written statements of the conditions that exist when a job is satisfactorily or adequately completed. They do not represent outstanding performance, or minimal performance, but rather satisfactory performance. There are certain criteria that should be followed in writing performance expectations. Once expectations have been written and agreed upon, the following Checklist can be used to see if they meet the necessary criteria:

EXPECTATIONS CHECKLIST

☐ "What to do" clearly stated

☐ "Satisfactory" performance clearly stated

☐ "Measurable" performance expectations

☐ Expectations "Jointly developed"

☐ Easily "interpreted" - clear

☐ "Reasonable" - Attainable

☐ Reviewed "frequently" / revised" if necessary

☐ Written with the "job" and the "person" in mind

EXPECTATIONS SHOULD BE ATTAINABLE

Expectations that are attainable become a motivating force towards greater productivity. If the expectation is perceived as unattainable or unrealistic, the person becomes discouraged or feels the expectation was really set for someone else's benefit.

GETTING COMMITMENT

As mentioned, Sales Managers should always be careful that the expectations set are "owned" by the Sales Rep. After all, it is the Sales Rep who is responsible for accomplishing them. For that reason, it's critical that you get the Sales Rep's commitment to meet them.

Getting commitment is really a process of getting the Sales Rep's involvement. If the Sales Rep has an influence in what will be accomplished, how and when it will be done, she or he will be committed to making it happen.

An example of getting commitment would be to try and get the Sales Person to commit to shooting for a higher sales volume, or to sell across the entire range of a product line.

Coming to agreed upon targets with your Sales Person is very similar to closing a sale when you were selling to customers. As such, you should follow the "A.I.PA." sequence.

It goes like this:

Attention: Use an attention-getting statement or question, such as, "How would you like to be the first person on the team to reach $100,000 in sales volume?"

Interest: Stress the benefits of hitting the new target. (i.e., increased earnings, recognition, pride, promotional opportunities, etc., etc.)

Presentation: Present some basic methods, techniques, tools, etc. that should enable your Sales Person to hit the targeted expectation.

Action: Ask for his/her commitment. "Close the sale."

SECTION 6: PRFORMANCE RATING CATAGORIES

Numerous articles and books have been written about the ideal number of rating catego- ries that Performance Appraisal Systems should use. The recommended numbers range from as few as three, to as many as ten ratings.

When arguing for three rating levels, Douglas McGregor in his book, *The Human Side of Enterprise observed:*

" . .it is probably safe to say that we can discriminate between the outstand- ingly good, the satisfactory and the unsatisfactory performers. When, however, we attempt to use the results of appraisals to make discriminations much finer than this, we are quite probably deluding ourselves."

The "Grandfather" of Performance Appraisals, Prof. Nathan B.Winstanley, of the University of Rochester agreed with McGregor in this quote from *The Conference Board Record* .

"Appraise and allocate the employee population into three descriptive catego- ries: (a) marginal, (b) competent, (c) exceptional, and award increases accord- ingly. Approximately 85% of the people should be appraised as competent. "

Prof. Winstanley reiterated his feelings about limiting rating categories to three in his statistical analysis of the relative degree of accuracy in this quote from an issue of *Personnel Administrator*:

"Error would be minimized if administrative distinctions were restricted to three categories only; say the bottom five percent (poor), the top five percent (outstanding) and all others in between (competent).

That, in essence, is exactly what McGregor said 40 years ago."

Reporting in the May/June 1988 issue of *The Harvard Business Review*

Saul Gellerman and William Hodgson indicated that American Cyanamid's experience with its new three rating system has been largely positive. Their ratings are S ("Superior"), Q ("Quality"), and N ("Needs Improvement"). Their previous system had allowed for ten possible ratings. They said the new system simplified the managers' appraisal tasks, and made determining and communicating ratings much easier. Not only did it cut managers' time spent preparing appraisals in half, it resulted in a "Surge" of favorable attitudes towards the new system.

Dr. Kenneth Apt of the Center for National Security Studies expressed a preference for four rating categories in his article in the January/February 1991 issue of *Corporate Controller*. He said:

"Five descriptors are easily misinterpreted as the five letter grades, and employees will consider them class rankings. The satisfactory/unsatisfactory route probably does not convey sufficient information to promote two-way communications. Four descriptors might be optimal: one indicating that expectations were surpassed, one conveying accomplishment, one indicating improvement is needed, and one reflecting failure to achieve performance standards.

"Communications are far more important than the descriptor itself, but employees tend to focus on the summary word or phrase. The challenge to you as a supervisor is to get the employee to understand what he or she did that met, surpassed or fell short of your expectations."

So, for the purposes of this booklet, we'll use four Performance Ratings. These ratings and their expected distribution over a large population of Sales People are:

PERFORMANCE RATINGS

DISTINGUISHED   (15% - 25%)

PROFICIENT   (50% - 60%)

DEVELOPMENTAL   (20% - 30%)

DEFICIENT   (0% - 5%)

The following is a definition of each of the ratings:

DISTINGUISHED

* Performance that is significantly beyond job requirements. * Exceptional achievement in key responsibilities.

* Excellent Performance in quality and quantity.

* Development relates to general business, cross-functional and/ or career opportunities.

PROFICIENT

* Performance that fulfills all job requirements. * Goes beyond expectations in many areas.

* Demonstrates a thorough knowledge and understanding of the position.

* Development relates to performance enhancement and/or future career opportunities.

DEVELOPMENTAL

* Performance that meets minimum job requirements.

* Expectations met in most areas/need improvement in others. * Key responsibilities are carried out satisfactorily.

* Further improvement is expected over time.

* Appropriate for a first review or longer term employees who have areas for improvement.

* Development relates to areas to improve performance and/ or encourage individual growth in current position.

DEFICIENT

* Job requirements not being met satisfactorily. * Failure to carry out key responsibilities.

* Continued performance at this level is not acceptable. * Significant improvement in the near future is required.

Or, it could result in reassignment or termination.

* Development relates to immediate attainment of minimum job performance level.

* Requires a documented corrective action plan.

SECTION 7: CONDUCTING EFFECTIVE PERFORMANCE PLANNING.

FEEDBACK AND APPRAISAL SESSIONS

Performance discussions are the most important opportunities Sales Managers have to help their Sales Reps, themselves and their companies. Done correctly, performance discussions are valuable tools in closing the gap between the actual performance of Sales Reps and the performance needed to meet corporate objectives.

As discussed in American Media Incorporated's Training Video, "The Human Touch Performance Appraisal," Performance Appraisals can be compared to an annual physical examination; both provide an opportunity for an honest assessment of how a person is doing. Sales People need to know what they're doing right so they can continue those activities. And, they also need to know what changes, if any, they need to make. People expect their doctor to be honest and specific. And, as their Sales Manager, your Sales Reps expect the same thing.

There is more to a performance appraisal than just filling out a form. Ideally, a performance appraisal is an ongoing event. If their Sales Managers give Sales Reps instant feedback on the jobs they've done throughout the year, performance appraisals are merely a summary of those events - and a projection of where those Sales People should be a year from now.

Sales Managers get the most from their Sales Reps when they sincerely listen to them and care about their hopes, dreams, and concerns. You can be the most knowledgeable and expert Sales Manager in the world, but people won't care how much you *KNOW* until they *KNOW* how much you care about them and their problems. By encouraging Sales Reps to build on their strengths, Sales Managers will help them to reach their true potential.

By putting the emphasis on completing the performance appraisal form, many sales managers miss the opportunity to show that they really care. They often miss the most important point in conducting performance appraisals:

<u>THE MOST IMPORTANT POINT IN CONDUCTING PERFORMANCE APPRAISALS IS SINCERELY CARING ABOUT YOUR SALES PEOPLE</u>

PERFORMANCE PLANNING MEETING

The Position/Job Description documents major job responsibilities and critical job elements. But often the tasks and goals and, therefore, the Sales Manager's expectations, are more specific - related to current conditions, problems, and plans. It is, therefore, necessary to communicate current expectations. These expectations should be expressed as goals, objectives, expected results or approaches. The establishment of performance expectations is a discussion, or series of discussions, in which the Sales Manager and the Sales Person reach agreement on how the Sales Person's performance will be evaluated over the performance period. The following Action Steps are suggested:

Action Steps

1. Discuss and agree on performance expectations for each of the Sales Person's major responsibilities.

2. Determine the steps the Sales Person will take to meet expectations, and ask for commitment.

3. Discuss Developmental Planning and Progress Review dates.

4. Indicate your availability to help the Sales Person if needed.

5. Express your confidence in the Sales Person's ability to achieve expectations, accomplish developmental plans, and set a date for a performance feedback discussion.

Ideally, each Sales Person should feel a sense of ownership of all expectations and developmental plans. This is achieved by encouraging Sales Rep participation in creating expectations and developmental action plans and a thorough discussion of them.

TIPS FOR A SUCCESSFUL PLANNING MEETING

❏   Prepare ahead of time to communicate the expected results you want.

❏   Plan to get participation from the Sales Person.

❏   Be flexible, versatile and not too rigid.

❏   Compromise where appropriate.

❏   Keep the discussion relaxed and "low key."

❏   Reduce tension to prevent confrontations.

❏   Keep your "cool."

❏   Remember: "**D**anger" is one letter away from "Anger."

PERIODIC FEEDBACK DISCUSSION

The Sales Manager and the Sales Rep need to dedicate some time periodically to step back from the daily activities and discuss the Rep's performance.

Periodic discussions allow the Sales Manager to reinforce good work, motivate corrective action where necessary, adjust the expectations as conditions change, and avoid surprises at appraisal time.

The Sales Rep is motivated and feels secure when kept informed, given a chance to discuss difficulties encountered, and given time to correct problems before appraisal time. The Sales Manager also has the opportunity to re-examine the expectations along the way and adjust them as appropriate.

Action Steps

1. Ask the Sales Rep to review progress to date for each responsibility and performance expectation.

2. Review each expectation separately.

3. Reinforce the positive results achieved.

4. Discuss Sales Rep acknowledged areas in need of improvement.

5. Discuss and resolve any areas of discrepancy ensuring that all factors have been considered.

6. Revise any responsibility and/or expectation where there has been a change within the job.

7. Review Developmental Action Plan and Progress Review dates.

8. Set a date for the next feedback session.

TIPS FOR A SUCCESSFUL FEEDBACK DISCUSSION

☐ Schedule it ahead of time.
☐ Ask the Sales Person to be thinking about performance towards targeted expectations.
☐ Cover only one thing at a time.
☐ Compare actual results with agreed upon expectations.
☐ Discuss Sales Person's Development.
☐ Close on a friendly note.
☐ Encourage them to keep up the good work.
☐ At all times, maintain and enhance their self-esteem.

CONDUCTING A FORMAL APPRAISAL

I. PREPARING THE SALES PERSON FOR THE APPRAISAL

The appraisal is the culmination of the performance period. It is the official point of contact with the compensation system and the communication of the Sales Rep's performance to higher management. Managing performance in this manner should lead to a comfortable, thoroughly anticipated evaluation and a constructive interview. There should be no surprises, for the Sales Rep or the Sales Manager.

The effectiveness of the appraisal session is highly influenced by both the Sales Manager and the Sales Rep being thoroughly prepared. These actions steps are recommended:

Action Steps

1. Review the process with the Sales Rep.

2. Ask the Sales Rep to complete and return a copy of the performance appraisal form. This self-appraisal is an essential part of the process.

3. Review the definitions of the performance ratings.

4. Discuss Developmental Planning.

5. Set a date for the appraisal within four to six weeks.

The Sales Manager should be completing a preliminary appraisal form during this period. Once your part is completed, ask the Sales Rep to return their self-appraisal to you. It is important for the Sales Manager's appraisal to **not** merely be a reaction to the Sales Rep's evaluation. As a Sales Manager, you may be including observations or information the Sales Rep has not considered.

TIPS FOR PREPARING SALES PEOPLE FOR APPRAISALS

☐ Based on their experience with appraisals, give them an appropriate overview of the process.

☐ Share with them company guidelines, manuals or this booklet.

☐ Keep the discussion appropriately relaxed to reduce their tension.

☐ Ask them to rate their own performance and provide specific, quantifiable justification for the ratings.

CONDUCTING A FORMAL APPRAISAL

II. CONDUCTING THE APPRAISAL SESSION

After completing your own preliminary appraisal form, compare your assessment with the one your Sales Rep submitted, and resolve areas of discrepancy by meeting with the Sales Rep, if necessary.

Complete the final appraisal form, review the appraisal with your manager, and obtain all necessary approvals from the compensation department for your salary recommendation.

You are now ready to meet with your Sales Rep for the appraisal interview. In this meeting, you will give your ratings on all the responsibilities, your overall rating, and the salary adjustment, if appropriate. Some companies prefer to separate the performance discussion from the salary discussion by a few weeks or so. This enables the Performance Appraisal to focus on performance and development, rather than placing too much emphasis on salary increases. You will also discuss the Sales Rep's development needs and agree on a specific action plan with progress review dates.

The tone of the meeting should be conversational and developmental. The following action steps are suggested:

Action Steps

1. Review each expectation separately.

2. Reinforce the positive results achieved.

3. Discuss Sales Rep-acknowledged areas in need of improvement.

4. Discuss and resolve any areas of discrepancy ensuring that all factors have been considered.

5. Give your overall rating and the salary adjustment, if appropriate.

6. Ask for the Sales Rep's ideas on development needs.

7. Agree on a specific Developmental Action Plan with Progress Review Dates.

8. Have the Sales Rep sign the Performance Appraisal form.

9. Set a date for a Performance Planning Meeting and Development Progress Review.

Allow enough time for this meeting so the Sales Rep can respond to comments and ratings and so the development plans can be jointly created.

TIPS FOR A SUCCESSFUL APPRAISAL MEETING

- ☐ Establish and maintain a friendly rapport at the beginning of the meeting.
- ☐ Set aside at least one and a half hours of uninterrupted time.
- ☐ Get away from the office, phone or other distractions.
- ☐ Encourage your Sales Rep to talk.
- ☐ Practice "Active Listening."
- ☐ Paraphrase back what your Sales Person has told you.
- ☐ Good feedback includes both your content and feelings.
- ☐ Utilize the communications style with which your Sales Rep feels most comfortable.
- ☐ Do all you can to reduce their tension.
- ☐ Evaluate on the basis of recent, accurate and specific information.
- ☐ Be honest, candid, and be prepared to discuss questionable items.
- ☐ Avoid comments on age, race, sex, religion, national origin, marital status, disabilities, etc. that may violate discrimination laws.
- ☐ Keep oral comments and written statements consistent.
- ☐ Make completed Appraisal available for Sales Person.
- ☐ Provide a right of appeal.
- ☐ Conclude on a positive note.

APPRAISAL SKILLS PARALLEL SELLING SKILLS

The skills that helped you sell well and were probably linked to your promotion to Sales Manager should be very useful in planning and conducting performance appraisals. Like selling, the skills needed to do Performance Reviews include:

SELLING AND APPRAISING SKILLS

1. Building Rapport
2. Identifying Needs
3. Questioning and Probing
4. Active Listening
5. Confirming
6. Maintaining a Contagious Enthusiasm
7. Keeping a Positive Attitude
8. Closing on Commitments

SALES PERSON GUIDELINES

WHAT SALES PEOPLE CAN DO TO HELP

Effective performance appraisals encourage two-way communications and place equal responsibility on the Sales Manager and the Sales Person. It should be a partnership effort that involves a spirit of cooperation and teamwork.

The Sale Rep's responsibility involves helping to think through the content of his or her position description and helping construct responsibility statements and performance expectations. Sales Reps have the responsibility for providing their Sales Managers with accurate information about their performance, preparing themselves for feedback sessions, the performance appraisal, preparing self-development recommendations and ensuring that the discussions take place at the right times.

When responsibilities and expectations have been jointly established and understood and when there is shared responsibility for all aspects of the appraisal process, it can be developmental for both parties.

Four to six weeks prior to appraisal date, Sales Reps should be asked to evaluate their own work using the performance appraisal form. Meanwhile, Sales Managers should be completing their own appraisal form on the Sales Person's performance. Then the two appraisals should be compared and any discrepancies resolved.

By using the guidelines below, Sales Managers and Sales People should be able to maximize the benefits of each performance discussion:

Sales Person Guidelines

1. Keep yourself and your Sales Manager focused on behavior and specifics.

2. Reinforce areas of agreement and ways in which your Sales Manager has been helpful.

3. When there's a discrepancy, acknowledge the Sales Manager's point of view and support your position with facts.

4. To clarify and ensure understanding, restate your Sales Manager's point of view.

5. Make sure feedback discussions are scheduled.

6. Provide your Sales Manager with feedback on how he or she can be more effective or provide you with better support and development.

TIPS FOR SALES PEOPLE BEING APPRAISED

(The following tips are reproduced in Section 14: Forms.
These may be photocopied and distributed to your Sales Reps)

- ❏ Don't get defensive or argumentative.
- ❏ Express appreciation for the way your Sales Manager has helped you and supported your efforts.
- ❏ Make it a pleasant experience for both parties.
- ❏ Discuss specific behaviors and results achieved.
- ❏ Help keep the focus on ways to enhance future performance through skills development.
- ❏ Accept feedback graciously and with appreciation.
- ❏ Practice "Active Listening."
- ❏ Paraphrase back what your Sales Manager has told you.
- ❏ Utilize the communications style with which your Sales Manager feels most comfortable.
- ❏ Do all you can to reduce his or her tension.
- ❏ The preservation of a good relationship between you and your boss should be your **"Number One Priority"**.
- ❏ Keep your cool.
- ❏ Remember: "**D**anger" is one letter away from "Anger."

SECTION 8: DEVELOPMENT PLANNING

To have a positive influence on future performance, a performance management program should place at least equal emphasis on mapping out future behaviors instead of devoting most of the time looking at past performance.

After the performance appraisal year is over, performance for that time period has, for the most part, been concluded.

Now, at annual appraisal time, it's the Sales Manager's responsibility to rate past performance on the expectations, give the overall rating, communicate the salary adjustment and move as quickly as possible into Developmental Recommendations designed to enhance future performance.

This step should be done in writing with projected targeted completion dates for each intervention agreed upon by the Sales Manager and the Sales Rep.

The development of their Sales People should be one of the most important responsibilities on every Sales Manager's position/job description.

A "Developmental Planning Guide" is provided to help in selecting training and development activities needed. This Guide can be used by Sales Managers to assist them in completing Developmental Action Plans with their Sales Reps. Types of Training & Development activities that should be considered are:

> * On-The-Job Work Experience
> * Formal Training Programs (Internal/External)
> * Formal Education (Undergraduate & Graduate)
> * Books, Speakers, Audio/Visual Cassettes, CD's and DVD's, Magazines, Clubs, Activities.

The following guide is provided to demonstrate the wide variety of developmental areas one can work towards.

Developmental Planning Guide

This Guide is provided to assist you in completing the Development Recommendations portion of the Performance Appraisal. Review each section of the Guide to identify areas the employee needs to develop and summarize this information on the Performance Appraisal.

I. PROFESSIONAL/MANAGERIAL AREAS

A. COMMUNICATIONS
- Oral
- Written
- Formal Presentation
- Listening

B. INTERPERSONAL
- Teamwork/Cooperation
- Influencing
- Negotiating
- Conflict Resolution
- Accepting and Dealing with Differing Viewpoints
- Maintaining Others' Self-Esteem
- Building Mutually Supportive and Trusting Relationships

C. ADMINISTRATIVE
- Planning
- Organizing
- Prioritizing
- Time Management
- Follow-up/Control
- Budgeting
- Proofreading
- Telephone Protocol
- Customer Service

D. HUMAN RESOURCE MANAGEMENT
- Interviewing and Selecting
- Labor Relations
- EEO/Affirmative Action
- Teambuilding
- Faciliating/Consulting
- Utilizing Personnel Effectively (Organization, Delegation, Staffing Level)
- Setting Ambitious but Realistic Goals/Objectives
- Establishing and Maintaining Performance Standards
- Providing Effective Performance Feedback
- Taking Corrective Action/Performance Improvement Planning
- Development Planning and Follow Through with Subordinates
- Coaching and Counseling
- Maintaining a Balance Between Concern for People and Concern for Work Production
- Teaching Others

E. LEADERSHIP
- Articulating and Instilling the Company's Vision
- Building and Maintaining Credibility
- Modifying Style to be Appropriate for Each Situation
- Seeking the Ideas and Opinions of Others
- Securing the Right Resources to Accomplish Objectives
- Building Functional/Cross-Functional Teams
- Encouraging Participative Management
- Making Effective Decisions Under the Pressures of Time and Limited Information
- Establishing a Climate of Trust and Mutual Respect
- Empowering Others with the Authority to Make Decisions
- Motivating Others by Appropriate Recognition and Constructive Feedback
- Deriving Satisfaction from Accomplishments of Others
- Inspiring Commitment to Goals and Action Plans
- Communicating Unpleasant News When Necessary
- Finding Ways to Get the Job Done When Normal Methods Will Not Work
- Building Confidence and Self-Esteem in Others
- Leading by Example
- Continuing Self Development

F. ANALYTICAL
- Assimilating Information
- Quantitative Analysis
- Problem Solving
- Creative Thinking

G. STRATEGIC
- Identifying Opportunities
- Grasping Interrelationships
- Anticipating Problems and Developing Alternative Solutions
- Integrating Strategies and Tactics/Positioning
- Focusing on Long-Term Effectiveness
- Understanding Organization Culture
- Exercising Appropriate Business Judgment

H. PERSONAL BEHAVIORAL DIMENSIONS
- Initiative
- Drive
- Perseverance
- Dedication/Commitment
- Perceptiveness
- Sensitivity
- Flexibility
- Resourcefulness
- Adaptability
- Patience
- Stress Management
- Risk Taking
- Achievement Oriented
- Entrepreneurial

DEVELOPMENTAL PLANNING GUIDE

II. TECHNICAL/FUNCTIONAL AREAS

I. TECHNICAL
- Food Technology
- Equipment Handling and Operations
- Statistical Process Control
- Statistical Quality Control
- Variance Analysis
- Safety
- Baking Technology
- Manufacturing Systems
- Socio-Technical Systems
- Quality Assurance/Control Systems
- Sensory Evaluation
- Sanitation and ES
- Food Science and Analysis
- Regulatory
- R & D Systems
- Packaging and Materials Management
- Engineering Systems
- Distribution Systems
- Sales Systems
- Marketing Systems
- Financial Systems
- Human Resource Systems
- Microcomputer Software Applications
- Information Services Technologies

J. FUNCTIONAL
- Selling
- Merchandising
- Sales Management
- Sales Strategies

J. FUNCTIONAL, cond't.
- Account Management
- Market Research
- Marketing Strategies
- Advertising
- Consumer and Trade Promotions
- Portfolio Management
- Financial Management
- Human Resource Management
- Information Systems Management
- Quality Improvement
- Company History and Capabilities
- General Business Knowledge

III. CROSS-FUNCTIONAL AREAS

K. KNOWLEDGE
- Manufacturing
- Quality Assurance/Control
- Engineering
- Logistics
- Sales
- Marketing
- Research and Development
- Personnel
- Finance
- Information Services

L. EFFECTIVENESS
- Developing Integrated Goals
- Coordinating Major Activities and Initiatives
- Communicating Issues and Impacts
- Understanding Cross-Functional Implications of Actions
- Ensuring Participative Decision Making

TYPES OF TRAINING & DEVELOPMENT ACTIVITIES:

- **On-The-Job Work Experience**
- **Formal Training Programs (Internal/External)**
  Sources:
    - **Developmental Matrix**
    - **Management Development & Training**
    - **Resource Guides**

- **Formal Education to Include Undergraduate and Graduate Technical and Business Courses (e.g., MBA Program)**

- **Other Sources: Books, Speakers, Audio/Visual Cassettes, Magazines, Clubs, Activities**

If you need assistance in identifying programs or development activities, please contact your manager or Human Resources Professional.

TIPS FOR SUCCESSFUL DEVELOPMENTAL PLANNING

❑ Sales people should describe for themselves <u>What</u> and <u>How</u> they should be working to improve.

❑ Rough drafts of the Developmental Section should be prepared by both parties prior to the meeting.

❑ Both people should be mutually committed to the Development Plan to ensure its completion.

❑ Continued learning throughout a person's life prevents stagnation and makes them more valuable to their employer.

SECTION 9: SELF EVALUATION TEST

One of the most critical aspects of the appraisal process should come prior to your beginning the process. This is where you have the opportunity to evaluate yourself. Make sure you are approaching the process with some balanced perspectives. Make sure you give each sale person's appraisal the thoughtful consideration it deserves.

A brief Self Evaluation Test follows. It was suggested in an article by Bill Stiles in the October 1990 issue of Agency Sales Magazine. Take the test and determine whether or not you approach the appraisal process in an equitable manner.

SELF EVALUATION TEST	YES	NO	SOME TIMES
1. Do you search for the reasons why Sales People perform the way they do?	5	-5	2
2. Are you able to suggest changes without sounding critical?	5	-2	2
3. Can you accept the unpleasant aspects of being a Sales Manager?	5	-2	2
4. Do you encourage your Sales People to fully express themselves?	5	-2	2
5. Are you always calm, regardless of circumstances?	5	-2	2
6. Do you compliment before approaching trouble areas and then follow with another compliment?	10	-5	5
7. Are you sure to always show respect for the individual?	5	-2	2
8. When you make a mistake, do you "own" it and correct it?	5	-2	2
9. Do you work with a Sales Person to arrive at a mutual plan?	10	-5	5

Add up the "Yes" points and "Sometimes" points. Subtract the "No" answers.

POINTS:
41-55 Excellent - You're already successful.
26-40 Fair - Work on your approaches.
16-25 Poor - Take some courses in Sales Mgmt.
0-15 Disaster - Pick another line of work.

SECTION 10: DO'S AND DON'TS OF PERFORMANCE APPRAISALS

DO'S AND DON'TS

(From American Media Incorporated's Training Video,
"The Human Touch Performance Appraisal")

DO THE FOLLOWING:

1. Reassure employees by building on their strengths.

2. Use a "We" approach when discussing problems.

3. Be specific when talking about performance.

4. Keep the discussions on track.

5. Draw them out by asking open-ended questions. Then listen to them.

6. Talk about results and accomplishments, not activities.

7. Serve as a coach, not a judge or police officer.

8. Close the discussion properly. Summarize, plan for improved performance and write down results.

BUT DON'T:

1. Use too many negative words or negative criticisms.

2. Use a "You vs. me" approach.

3. Give insincere of excessive praises.

4. Use generalities that can't be backed up by specifics.

5. Dominate the entire conversation.

6. Place emphasis on personality or attitudes.

7. Rush or seem hurried.

8. Demonstrate a condescending nature.

Remember, this is the most important business day of the year for your Sales Person. It's their time in the spotlight. They deserve this uninterrupted time with their Sales Manager. It should be free from all distractions and outside interferences. It should be as pleasant an experience as possible.

SECTION 11: EXAMPLES OF MEASURABLE EXPECTATIONS

Listed below are some examples of measurable expectations that could be used for sales positions at each level of the performance ratings discussed earlier:

EXPECTATION	RATING
Exceed Quota on Widget Sales:	
10 units over quota & higher	Distinguished
Plus or minus 9 units of quota	Proficient
10 to 20 units under quota	Developmental
21 units or more under quota	Deficient
Achieve Monthly Objectives Parameters:	
10 - 12 Months	Distinguished
8 - 9 Months	Proficient
6 - 7 Months	Developmental
5 months or fewer	Deficient
Maintains 50% of Distributors:	
55% to 100%	Distinguished
45% to 54.9%	Proficient
35% to 44.9%	Developmental
0% to 34.9%	Deficient
Maintain or Increase Market Share:	
+20% and greater	Distinguished
0% to +19.9%	Proficient
-20% to - 0.9%	Developmental
-20.1% and lower	Deficient
Collections on Past Due Accounts:	
90% to 100%	Distinguished
70% to 89.9%	Proficient
50% to 69.9%	Developmental
49.9% and below	Deficient
New Widget Varieties Sold:	
90% to 100%	Distinguished
70% to 89.9%	Proficient
50% to 69.9%	Developmental
49.9% and below	Deficient

SECTION 12: QUESTIONS AND ANSWERS

SOME COMMON QUESTIONS OFTEN RELATED TO
PERFORMANCE APPRAISALS ARE:

Q.   How often is someone evaluated?

A.   Each person's performance should be formally appraised annually.
     During the performance appraisal, a rating of the past year's
     contributions against expectations should be made. This is
     also the proper time to discuss base salary increases, if appropriate.

Q.   When does performance feedback occur?

A.   Performance feedback should occur periodically during the year to
     discuss job responsibilities and expectations, current performance,
     positive and negative, market conditions, competitive activity,
     and make adjustments in the expectations as needed.

Q.   Can a Sales Person institute a performance feedback
     discussion?

A.   Yes. An effective performance management system emphasizes that
     feedback is a two-way communications arrangement. A Sales
     Manager and Sales Rep are encouraged to have open lines of
     communications to ensure formal and informal feedback when
     appropriate during the year.

Q.   Why is someone evaluated?

A.   Sales People are appraised on their performance to:

     *   Promote better understanding between Sales Managers
         and Sales People about the organization's
         performance expectations and the means for achieving them.

     *   Motivate Sales Reps to achieve higher levels of performance.

     *   Link increases to base pay when performance expectations are
         achieved and/or exceeded.

     *   Enhance Sales Force morale by giving timely feedback
         and assistance in improving performance.

     *   Support Sales Rep development with specific developmental action
         plans and progress review dates.

Q.   What is a Position Description versus a Performance
      Expectation?

A.   The basic document of performance planning is the
      Position Description. It is created when an employee
      enters a new job, and it is reviewed each year. It is
      a relatively permanent document in that it describes the
      scope of responsibility and the specific job responsibilities.

      The Position Description documents the major
      responsibilities and critical job elements. Often
      the tasks and goals, and therefore the Sales Manager's
      expectations, are more specific, related to current
      market/customer conditions, competitive activities,
      problems, plans, etc. It is therefore necessary to
      communicate current expectations, expressing them
      in terms of the current environment. These expectations
      are, in essence, the current meanings of the
      responsibilities, expressed as goals, objectives,
      or approaches.

Q.   Why are performance appraisals secret?

A.   Performance management is not intended to be a "secret"
      program. Sales Managers and Sales Reps are encouraged
      to learn all about and share all the information about
      a company's performance evaluation policies so they
      can have a shared understanding about them.

Q.   What recourse should Sales People have if they don't
      agree with their Sales Manager's appraisal of their performance?

A.   They can put down their comments under "Employee
      Comments" on the appraisal form, or provisions could
      be made for them to ask to see their boss's boss. But
      the best way to correct an inaccurate appraisal is
      to prevent one from happening. The best preventative
      for misunderstandings is frequent, ongoing
      communications about the job, the achievement of
      expectations and job performance against targeted
      objectives. Sales Reps have as much of a right to call
      meetings to discuss performance as managers do.

SECTION 13: BIBLIOGRAPHY

American Society for Training and Development's Infoline Booklet "How to Conduct a Performance Appraisal" May, 1990.

Apt, Kenneth E., "Performance Appraisal - How to Get It Right" Corporate Controller, January/February, 1991.

Evans, Elaine M., "Designing an Effective Performance Management System" Journal of Compensation and Benefits, March/April, 1991.

Gellerman, Saul W., and Hodgson, William G., "Cyanamid's New Take on Performance Appraisal" Harvard Business Review, May/June, 1988.

Graham, Gerald, "Managers Often Vague in Defining Goals to Workers" Morristown, N.J. Daily Record Newspaper, May 18, 1988.

Losyk, Bob, "Face to Face: How to Conduct an Employee Appraisal Interview" Credit Union Executive Magazine, Winter 1990-1991.

Martin, D.C., "The Legal Ramifications of Performance Appraisal" Employee relations Law Journal, Vol. 12, No. 2, 1986.

McGregor, Douglas, The Human Side of Enterprise, McGraw Hill, 1960.

Pratt, Henry J., "Principles of Effective Performance Management" Records Management Quarterly, January, 1991.

Stiles, Bill, "Agents: How to Evaluate Your Sales Personnel" Agency Sales Magazine, October, 1990."

"The Human Touch Performance Appraisal" (Training Video) American Media Incorporated, 1991.

Townley, Barbara, "A Discriminating Approach to Appraisal" Personnel Management, December, 1990.

Winstanley, Nathan B., "How Accurate are Performance Appraisals?" Personnel Administrator, August, 1980.

Winstanley, Nathan B., "The Use of Performance Appraisal in Compensation Administration" The Conference Board Record, March, 1975.

SECTION 14: SAMPLE FORMS COMPLETED

Sample Forms
Completed

The Following Are Sample Appraisal Forms As Completed For One Hypothetical Individual. This Set Demonstrates How the Performance Information Flows Throughout The Appraisal Process.

POSITION DESCRIPTION/REQUISITION

POSITION TITLE _____Sales Rep_____ INCUMBENT'S NAME ____John Doe____

COMPONENT ____Widget Central____ LOCATION _____ EFFECTIVE DATE _____

MANAGER'S TITLE _____Sales Manager_____ NAME _____

DESCRIBE THE BROAD FUNCTION AND SCOPE OF THE POSITION:

> Responsible for attainment of assigned sales quotas by selling across the entire range of the product line. Maintain solid customer relations with all customers to ensure customer satisfaction and repeat business. Maintain and improve market shares through aggressive and innovative selling and marketing techniques.

DESCRIBE THE PRINCIPAL CONTINUING RESPONSIBILITIES OF THE POSITION IN ORDER OF IMPORTANCE:

1. Plan and implement sales and marketing strategies in all classes of accounts on assigned territory to exceed monthly sales quotas of Widgets.

2. Balance sales and delivery schedules in order to achieve monthly objectives for each month of the year.

3. Achieve Distributor Account objectives in order to maintain and maximize this classification of account throughout the year.

4. Perform all administrative tasks so that reports are sub-mitted on time, account records are posted regularly, computer and delivery efficiency are maintained and operations guidelines are adhered to.

5. Ensure that our customers are fully informed of operating policies, prices, new Widget varieties, etc.

6. Assist management with sales meetings, training new Sales Reps, preparing expense budgets, and other special projects on an as-needed basis.

Performance Appraisal

NAME: **John Doe**   REVIEW PERIOD FROM: **Jan.** TO: **Dec.**

TITLE: **Sales Rep**   COMPONENT: **Widget Central**

RESPONSIBILITIES & PERFORMANCE EXPECTATIONS	PERFORMANCE COMMENTS	Distinguished	Proficient	Developmental	Deficient
Sales Over Widget Quotas: 10 units over + — Distinguished Plus or minus 9 — Proficient -10 to -20 under — Developmental -21 units plus — Deficient	John achieved a sales level of 17 units over his Widget quota from January to December.	X			
Monthly Objectives Parameters: 10 - 12 Months — Distinguished 8 - 9 Months — Proficient 6 - 7 Months — Developmental 5 Months or fewer — Deficient	John achieved his monthly objective 8 times this year. However, he had 1 account close and 1 account go bankrupt in the first quarter.		X		
Maintains 50% of Distributors: 55% to 100% — Distinguished 45% to 54.9% — Proficient 35% to 44.9% — Developmental 0% to 34.9% — Deficient	The maintenance of Distributor Accounts averaged 61.5% throughout the year.	X			
Market Share Increases: +20% & greater — Distinguished 0% to 19.9% — Proficient -20% to -0.9% — Developmental -20.1% & Lower — Deficient	Territory showed a 16.8% increase in market shares for Widgets over the same period last year.		X		
Past Due Collections: 90% to 100% — Distinguished 70% to 89.9% — Proficient 50% to 69.9% — Developmental 49.9% & Lower — Deficient	95% of all past due accounts were collected during acceptable time frames.	X			
New Widget Variety Placements: 90% to 100% — Distinguished 70% to 89.9% — Proficient 50% to 69.9% — Developmental 49.9% & Lower — Deficient	John averaged a 92.7% placement ratio on all new Widget varieties during the year.	X			

PERFORMANCE RATING		Distinguished	Proficient	Developmental	Deficient
RESPONSIBILITIES & PERFORMANCE EXPECTATIONS	**PERFORMANCE COMMENTS**				
Administrative Performance: 1. Reports submitted on time. 2. Computer efficiency. 3. Posting of sales records. 4. Operation guidelines. 5. Delivery efficiency.	- 2 late reports. - no computer errors. - posts sales records daily. - 4 special deliveries due to Widgets being out-of-stock		X		

PERFORMANCE SUMMARY

John continues to be a team leader in overall Widget sales, new Widget varieties, and winning contests. He has also voluntarily taken over as the lead coach for newly hired Widget Sales Reps. He is also the team leader in market share increases and collections from past due accounts. He made four excellent presentations at the quarterly sales meetings.

		OVERALL RATING	X		

DEVELOPMENT RECOMMENDATIONS

AREAS _{REFER TO DEVELOPMENTAL PLANNING GUIDE}	ACTION PLANS _{TRAINING PROGRAMS, JOB ASSIGNMENTS, COACHING ACTIVITIES}	PROGRESS REVIEW DATE
PROFESSIONAL/MANAGERIAL To improve listening skills.	1. Listening to selling/communications tapes and videos from the company tape rental library and attend an Active Listening seminar.	By end of 1st quarter
TECHNICAL/FUNCTIONAL Learn new computer applications and train new reps. How to use them.	1. Work one week with the company analyst to learn new systems. 2. Make 2 presentations at meetings.	By end of 2nd quarter
CROSS/FUNCTIONAL Work closer with warehouse in order to reduce Widget out-of-stocks that require special deliveries.	1. Spend one day with warehouse manager and one day in distribution office to learn scheduling techniques.	By end of the year

APPRAISER SIGNATURE *Mary Johnson*	DATE Nov. 30	APPROVAL SIGNATURE *Ralph Smith*	DATE DEC 15
EMPLOYEE SIGNATURE *John Doe*			

EMPLOYEE COMMENTS

Very well done appraisal. I will work on my development recommendations.

Performance Factors Worksheet

	Distinguished	Proficient	Developmental	Deficient	Not Observed	Not Applicable
1. PROBLEM SOLVING						
a. Shows good judgment	✓					
b. Makes timely and fact-based decisions		✓				
c. Handles pressure situations		✓				
COMMENTS *Uses excellent problem solving skills in dealing with customers.*						
2. OUTPUT						
a. Quantity of output	✓					
b. Quality of output	✓					
c. Meets deadlines			✓			
COMMENTS *Quantity & quality of sales output and need & budget variation sold is above average. Needs to work on delivery efficiency & getting reports in on time.*						
3. VERSATILITY						
a. Tries new ideas	✓					
b. Responds to change	✓					
c. Innovative	✓					
d. Utilizes internal and external resources		✓				
COMMENTS *Extremely versatile individual. Could get better utilization from warehouse operations and distribution office.*						
4. JOB KNOWLEDGE						
a. Keeps abreast of advances in individual's function and related functions		✓				
b. Has working knowledge of other related functions		✓				
COMMENTS *Should work closer with Company Analyst to master new Computer system.*						

	Distinguished	Proficient	Developmental	Deficient	Not Observed	Not Applicable
5. PLANNING						
a. Anticipates events				✓		
b. Develops thorough plans			✓			
c. Prepares contingency plans			✓			
d. Sets clear and measurable goals		✓				
e. Understands/Sets priorities				✓		
f. Allocates time effectively				✓		
g. Delegates authority appropriately				✓		

COMMENTS Sets clear and measurable sales goals and new widget varieties goals. Needs to anticipate demand better to reduce out-of-stock conditions.

	Distinguished	Proficient	Developmental	Deficient	Not Observed	Not Applicable
6. CONTROL						
a. Sets control points in terms of time, dollars, budget		✓				
b. Follows up to ensure actions taken	✓					
c. Responds to changing conditions involving people and events		✓				

COMMENTS Adept at setting follow-up plans to ensure actions are taken.

	Distinguished	Proficient	Developmental	Deficient	Not Observed	Not Applicable
7. LEADERSHIP						
a. Motivates others		✓				
b. Selects competent subordinates						✓
c. Trains/develops subordinates		✓				
d. Seeks and accepts responsibility		✓				
e. Inspires morale of subordinates		✓				
		✓				

COMMENTS A team leader when it comes to training and coaching new widget Sales Reps.

	Distinguished	Proficient	Developmental	Deficient	Not Observed	Not Applicable
8. COMMUNICATION (Consider, openness, completeness, accuracy, clarity, timeliness and delivery)						
a. Written		✓				
b. Verbal - to subordinates						
c. Verbal - to peers	✓					
d. Verbal - to superiors	✓					
e. Group Presentations	✓					

COMMENTS One of the best group presenters on the team. Should work on developing his listening skills.

	Distinguished	Proficient	Developmental	Deficient	Not Observed	Not Applicable
9. TEAMWORK						
a. Cooperates with other departments, divisions, groups			✓			
b. Establishes rapport with others			✓			

COMMENTS Great with Sales People. Needs to establish some rapport with warehouse Operations and Distribution Office.

<u>CONDUCTING THE APPRAISAL SESSION</u>

<u>The general situation:</u>

John is one of the best performers on the team. He's distinguished by sales over widget Quotas, new widget variety placements, Contests, training new Reps and making presentations at meetings.

Needs to improve his listening skills, learn new computer applications and work to reduce widget out-of-stocks which makes special deliveries necessary.

<u>How will the Sales Rep react?</u>

No problem. He has been aware of his developmental needs for at least two years now. He does want a promotion, but realizes he has some improvements to make to earn it.

<u>What questions will the Sales Rep ask?</u>

How can I get promoted? How much more money am I going to make next year?

Why is it necessary to stay upon my paperwork as long as I'm hitting my sales numbers?

PREPARATION FOR CONDUCTING A FORMAL APPRAISAL

Please write down the comments you plan to make under each of the Action Steps:

ACTION STEPS

1. Preparing the Sales Rep for the Appraisal

   1. Review the process with the Sales Rep.

   John is quite familiar with the process – I plan to give him a copy of this booklet on "How to Plan & Conduct Performance Appraisals".

   2. Ask the Sales Rep to complete and return a copy of the Performance Appraisal form.

   I'll give him a copy of the Performance Appraisal form with the expectations we agreed to at the beginning of the year filled out on the left hand side. I'll ask him to fill in the "comments" for each expectation and rate each one accordingly. I'll give him two weeks

   3. Review the definitions of the performance ratings. *to return it to m*

   John knows the definitions, but I'll ask him to review them in the "How To" Booklet and make sure the comments justify the ratings.

   4. Discuss Developmental Planning.

   I'll ask him to be thinking about some developmental plans he'd like to undertake next year. He should turn in a rough draft of the plans when he gives me back his self-appraisal.

   5. Set a date for the appraisal within four to six weeks.

   I'll ask him to set aside Dec. 21st from 8:30 AM to 10:00 AM for his annual appraisal.

PREPARATION FOR CONDUCTING A FORMAL APPRAISAL (cont.)

Please write down the comments you plan to make under each of the Action Steps:

ACTION STEPS

1. Conducting the Appraisal Session

   1. Review each expectation separately.

      I plan to go over each expectation and first ask John how he thinks he's doing with each one.

   2. Reinforce the positive results achieved.

      I'll compliment him on all the expectations, particularly sales over widget quotas, distributors, Past due accounts & new widget varieties.

   3. Discuss Sales Rep-acknowledged areas in need of improvement.

      John knows he's got development needs in Paperwork, deliveries, listening skills and computer applications.

   4. Discuss and resolve any areas of discrepancy - ensuring that all factors have been considered.

      John will probably argue for a "Distinguished" on monthly objectives due to 1 account closing-1 going bankrupt.

   5. Give your overall rating and the salary adjustment, if appropriate.

      He should be very pleased with his over-all "Distinguished" rating.

   6. Ask for the Sales Rep's ideas on development needs.

      I'll ask for his commitment to complete the Development Plan.

   7. Agree on a specific Developmental Action Plan with Progress Review dates.

      I'm sure John will agree to the Plan, but we'll have to review it quarterly to ensure follow-up.

   8. Have the Sales Rep sign the Performance Appraisal form.

      John will sign it and probably make a favorable comment.

   9. Set a date for a Performance Planning Meeting and Development Progress Review

      I'll ask him to reserve Jan. 7th from 8:30 AM to 9:30 AM for a Performance Planning meeting for next year's Performance Objectives.

BOB KLEIN

Section15: Blank Forms

These blank forms
can be reproduced
for your own use,
compliments of

Professional Society for Sales and Marketing Training

POSITION DESCRIPTION/REQUISITION

POSITION TITLE _____INCUMBENT'S NAME _____

COMPONENT _____LOCATION _____ EFFECTIVE DATE _____

MANAGER'S TITLE _____NAME _____

DESCRIBE THE BROAD FUNCTION AND SCOPE OF THE POSITION:

DESCRIBE THE PRINCIPAL CONTINUING RESPONSIBILITIES OF THE POSITION IN ORDER OF IMPORTANCE:

Performance Appraisal

NAME: _____ REVIEW PERIOD FROM: _____ TO: _____

TITLE: _____ COMPONENT: _____

RESPONSIBILITIES & PERFORMANCE EXPECTATIONS	PERFORMANCE COMMENTS	Distinguished	Proficient	Developmental	Deficient

PERFORMANCE RATING		Distinguished	Proficient	Developmental	Deficient
RESPONSIBILITIES & PERFORMANCE EXPECTATIONS	**PERFORMANCE COMMENTS**				
Administrative Performance: 1. Reports submitted on time. 2. Computer efficiency. 3. Posting of sales records. 4. Operation guidelines. 5. Delivery efficiency.	- 2 late reports. - no computer errors. - posts sales records daily. - 4 special deliveries due to Widgets being out-of-stock		X		

PERFORMANCE SUMMARY

John continues to be a team leader in overall Widget sales, new Widget varieties, and winning contests. He has also voluntarily taken over as the lead coach for newly hired Widget Sales Reps. He is also the team leader in market share increases and collections from past due accounts. He made four excellent presentations at the quarterly sales meetings.

OVERALL RATING	X			

DEVELOPMENT RECOMMENDATIONS

AREAS REFER TO DEVELOPMENTAL PLANNING GUIDE	**ACTION PLANS** TRAINING PROGRAMS, JOB ASSIGNMENTS, COACHING ACTIVITIES	**PROGRESS REVIEW DATE**
PROFESSIONAL/MANAGERIAL To improve listening skills.	1. Listening to selling/communications tapes and videos from the company tape rental library and attend an Active Listening seminar.	By end of 1st quarter
TECHNICAL/FUNCTIONAL Learn new computer applications and train new reps. How to use them.	1. Work one week with the company analyst to learn new systems. 2. Make 2 presentations at meetings.	By end of 2nd quarter
CROSS/FUNCTIONAL Work closer with warehouse in order to reduce Widget out-of-stocks that require special deliveries.	1. Spend one day with warehouse manager and one day in distribution office to learn scheduling techniques.	By end of the year

APPRAISER SIGNATURE *Mary Johnson*	DATE *Nov. 30*	APPROVAL SIGNATURE *Ralph Smith*	DATE *Dec 15*

EMPLOYEE SIGNATURE *John Doe*

EMPLOYEE COMMENTS

Very well done appraisal. I will work on my development recommendations.

Performance Factors Worksheet

	Distinguished	Proficient	Developmental	Deficient	Not Observed	Not Applicable
1. PROBLEM SOLVING						
a. Shows good judgment						
b. Makes timely and fact-based decisions						
c. Handles pressure situations						
COMMENTS						
2. OUTPUT						
a. Quantity of output						
b. Quality of output						
c. Meets deadlines						
COMMENTS						
3. VERSATILITY						
a. Tries new ideas						
b. Responds to change						
c. Innovative						
d. Utilizes internal and external resources						
COMMENTS						
4. JOB KNOWLEDGE						
a. Keeps abreast of advances in individual's function and related functions						
b. Has working knowledge of other related functions						
COMMENTS						

	Distinguished	Proficient	Developmental	Deficient	Not Observed	Not Applicable
5. PLANNING						
a. Anticipates events						
b. Develops thorough plans						
c. Prepares contingency plans						
d. Sets clear and measurable goals						
e. Understands/Sets priorities						
f. Allocates time effectively						
g. Delegates authority appropriately						
COMMENTS						
6. CONTROL						
a. Sets control points in terms of time, dollars, budget						
b. Follows up to ensure actions taken						
c. Responds to changing conditions involving people and events						
COMMENTS						
7. LEADERSHIP						
a. Motivates others						
b. Selects competent subordinates						
c. Trains/develops subordinates						
d. Seeks and accepts responsibility						
e. Inspires morale of subordinates						
COMMENTS						
8. COMMUNICATION (Consider, openness, completeness, accuracy, clarity, timeliness and delivery)						
a. Written						
b. Verbal - to subordinates						
c. Verbal - to peers						
d. Verbal - to superiors						
e. Group Presentations						
COMMENTS						
9. TEAMWORK						
a. Cooperates with other departments, divisions, groups						
b. Establishes rapport with others						
COMMENTS						

CONDUCTING THE APPRAISAL SESSION

The general situation:

How will the Sales Rep react?

What questions will the Sales Rep ask?

PREPARATION FOR CONDUCTING A FORMAL APPRAISAL

Please write down the comments you plan to make under each of the Action Steps:

ACTION STEPS

1. Preparing the Sales Rep for the Appraisal

    1. Review the process with the Sales Rep.

    _____

    _____

    2. Ask the Sales Rep to complete and return a copy of the Performance Appraisal form.

    _____

    _____

    3. Review the definitions of the performance ratings.

    _____

    _____

    4. Discuss Developmental Planning.

    _____

    _____

    5. Set a date for the appraisal within four to six weeks.

    _____

    _____

PREPARATION FOR CONDUCTING A FORMAL APPRAISAL (cont.)

Please write down the comments you plan to make under each of the Action Steps:

ACTION STEPS

1. Conducting the Appraisal Session

    1. Review each expectation separately.

    _____

    _____

    2. Reinforce the positive results achieved.

    _____

    _____

    3. Discuss Sales Rep-acknowledged areas in need of improvement.

    _____

    _____

    4. Discuss and resolve any areas of discrepancy - ensuring that all factors have been considered.

    _____

    _____

    5. Give your overall rating and the salary adjustment, if appropriate.

    _____

    _____

    6. Ask for the Sales Rep's ideas on development needs.

    _____

    _____

    7. Agree on a specific Developmental Action Plan with Progress Review dates.

    _____

    _____

    8. Have the Sales Rep sign the Performance Appraisal form.

    _____

    _____

    9. Set a date for a Performance Planning Meeting and Development Progress Review

    _____

    _____

TIPS FOR SALES PEOPLE BEING APPRAISED

(This form may be photocopied and distributed to Sales Reps)

☐ Don't get defensive or argumentative.

☐ Express appreciation for the way your Sales Manager has helped you and supported your efforts.

☐ Make it a pleasant experience for both parties.

☐ Discuss specific behaviors and results achieved.

☐ Help keep the focus on ways to enhance future performance through skills development.

☐ Accept feedback graciously and with appreciation.

☐ Practice "Active Listening."

☐ Paraphrase back what your Sales Manager has told you.

☐ Utilize the communications style with which your Sales Manager feels most comfortable.

☐ Do all you can to reduce his or her tension.

☐ The preservation of a good relationship between you and your boss should be your **"Number One Priority."**

☐ Keep your cool.

☐ Remember: "**D**anger" is one letter away from "Anger."

SKILL USE PLAN
CONDUCTING A FORMAL APPRAISAL

Name: _____ Date:_____

_____

_____

Directions: You have just spent some time learning a new management skill. As is
true of any skill, performance will drop if the skill is not practiced. Therefore, please take a few minutes to decide when and with whom you will
use the skills taught in this booklet. After completing this Section of the
Skill Use Plan, use it to prepare for your planned discussion. This section
can be used in planning your meetings, and Section II can be used as a
self-critique after your discussion.

_____

_____

Skill Practice Preparation

Sales Rep's name: _____

Planned date of discussion: _____

_____

Specific meeting objective: _____

_____

Anticipated Sales Rep reaction: _____

_____

Your ideas for achieving the objective: _____

_____

SECTION II
Skill Practice Review

Actual date of discussion: _____

Action Steps Followed:

	Yes	No
I. Preparing the Sales Rep for the Appraisal		
1. Review the process with the Sales Rep.	_____	_____
2. Ask the Sales Rep to complete and return a copy of the Performance Appraisal form.	_____	_____
3. Review the definitions of the performance ratings.	_____	_____
4. Discuss Developmental Plans.	_____	_____
5. Set a date for the appraisal within four to six weeks.	_____	_____
II. Conducting the Appraisal Session		
1. Review each expectation separately.	_____	_____
2. Reinforce the positive results achieved.	_____	_____
3. Discuss Sales Rep-acknowledged areas in need of improvement.	_____	_____
4. Discuss and resolve any areas of discrepancy – ensuring that all factors have been considered.	_____	_____
5. Give your overall rating and the salary adjustment, if appropriate.	_____	_____
6. Ask for the Sales Rep's ideas on development needs.	_____	_____
7. Agree on a specific Developmental Action Plan with Progress Review dates.	_____	_____
8. Have the Sales Rep sign the Performance Appraisal form.	_____	_____
9. Set a date for a Performance Planning Meeting and Development Progress Review.	_____	_____
What was the Sales Rep's overall reaction to the discussion?	_____	_____

_____

_____

How did you feel after the discussion?

_____

_____

Notes

Notes

Notes

Notes

Notes

ABOUT THE AUTHOR

Bob Klein has retired after a 34 year career with Nabisco as Director of National Training, three years with Porter Henry & Company as a Vice President and five years with Wyeth  Pharmaceuticals as Director of Global Training. He also served as an Adjunct Professor at Cal. State Fullerton, UCLA and Philadelphia University. Bob has written two non-fiction books on Amazon: *"How To Make $1 Million Dollars F.A.S.T.: And Make It Last"* and *"From Cotton Picker To Multimillionaire: An Autobiography"*. The first is a self-help book and the latter is the true story of Bob's growing up poor in the South and his subsequent careers.

This is his third book. It's full of insights that would be helpful to anybody who would like to duplicate his "rags to riches" story.

www.ingramcontent.com/pod-product-compliance
Lightning Source LLC
Chambersburg PA
CBHW081552170526
45166CB00009B/2669